D1370484

BATS SET II

FRINGE-LIPPED BATS

Jill C. Wheeler
ABDO Publishing Company

GAS CITY–MILL TWP.
Public Library

visit us at
www.abdopub.com

Published by ABDO Publishing Company, 4940 Viking Drive, Edina, Minnesota 55435.
Copyright © 2006 by Abdo Consulting Group, Inc. International copyrights reserved in all
countries. No part of this book may be reproduced in any form without written permission from
the publisher. The Checkerboard Library™ is a trademark and logo of ABDO Publishing
Company.

Printed in the United States.

Cover Photo: Corbis
Interior Photos: Animals Animals p. 13; © Merlin D. Tuttle, Bat Conservation International
    pp. 5, 9, 11, 17, 19, 21

Series Coordinator: Tamara L. Britton
Editors: Tamara L. Britton, Stephanie Hedlund
Art Direction, Maps, and Diagrams: Neil Klinepier

Library of Congress Cataloging-in-Publication Data

Wheeler, Jill C., 1964-
    Fringe-lipped bats / Jill C. Wheeler.
        p. cm. -- (Bats. Set II)
    Includes index.
    ISBN 1-59679-321-X
     1. Fringe-lipped bat--Juvenile literature. I. Title.

    QL737.C57W489 2005
    599.4'5--dc22

                                                    2005045794

CONTENTS

FRINGE-LIPPED BATS

Fringe-lipped bats are one of more than 900 **species** of bats. Only rodents have more species than bats do. Of the many bat species, there are only ten that are **carnivorous**. Fringe-lipped bats are among these carnivorous bats.

All bats are **mammals**. Humans are mammals, too. Like humans, bats have backbones. Mother bats produce milk to feed their young just like human mothers do. However, bats are the only mammals that truly fly.

Many people think bats are scary or harmful to humans. This is not true. Bats prefer to avoid people.

They are very helpful because they eat many insect pests. They also help **pollinate** plants and re-plant forests. Humans and bats are important partners in Earth's **ecosystem**.

Fringe-lipped bats like to eat frogs. So, they are also called frog-eating bats.

WHERE THEY'RE FOUND

Bats are found all around the world. They live everywhere except for some **isolated** islands, and the North and South poles. Fringe-lipped bats live in the lowland tropical forests of the Americas.

In North America, they can be found in southern Mexico. From there they can be found in Central America, down to Bolivia and Brazil in South America. They also have been found on the island of Trinidad.

In all these places, fringe-lipped bats like to live near water. That is because of their favorite food. The frogs they like to eat live near water, too.

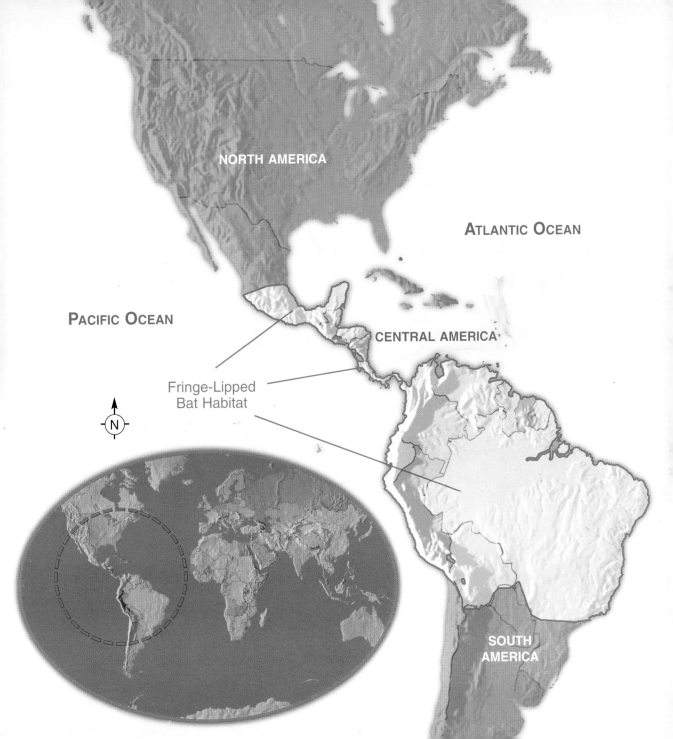

NORTH AMERICA

ATLANTIC OCEAN

PACIFIC OCEAN

CENTRAL AMERICA

Fringe-Lipped
Bat Habitat

N

SOUTH
AMERICA

WHERE THEY LIVE

Fringe-lipped bats live with other bats in a colony. A fringe-lipped bat colony usually has about six bats in it. One of the bats in the colony is male. The others are female.

Fringe-lipped bats are **nocturnal**. That means they hunt at night and sleep during the day. They like to **roost** in caves or hollow tree trunks. Sometimes, they share their roost with other bat **species**.

Fringe-lipped bats do not limit themselves to trees or caves. Researchers have found colonies in abandoned tunnels, **culverts**, and old buildings. One colony was even found on a coconut plantation!

Opposite page: *There are four bats in this colony, three females and one male. The male is at the bottom of the colony. One of the females is yawning!*

Sizes

Bats around the world come in all shapes and sizes. The smallest bat is Thailand's bumblebee bat. It is about the size of a large bumblebee.

The largest bats are called flying foxes. They are the world's largest flying **mammals**. Some **species** of flying foxes are more than 16 inches (41 cm) long. They can have a **wingspan** of more than 5 feet (1.5 m).

Fringe-lipped bats fall between these two extremes. They are medium-sized bats. Fringe-lipped bats grow to be about 4 inches (10 cm) long. They can weigh up to 1 ounce (28 g).

Like all bats, fringe-lipped bats are part of the order Chiroptera. This is a Greek word that means "hand wing." Bats have hands that are also wings! This fringe-lipped bat holds a frog in its hands while eating.

SHAPES

Fringe-lipped bats have thick, waterproof fur. It is dark brown, reddish brown, or grayish brown. Their undersides are a brown gray color.

Fringe-lipped bats have arms and hands, like humans do. Each hand has four long fingers, and a thumb with a claw. Their wings, or flight **membranes**, are dark brown. The wings stretch between their fingers, body, and legs. Fringe-lipped bats have large feet with strong claws. Their tail is small.

Fringe-lipped bats have big ears that are longer than their heads. They have long whiskers. And, they have sharp teeth for catching **prey**. They also have another feature that helps them hunt. Wartlike bumps cover their lips and **muzzle**. These bumps are called dermal denticles, or skin teeth. Researchers believe the bats use them to sense poisonous frogs.

Bat Anatomy

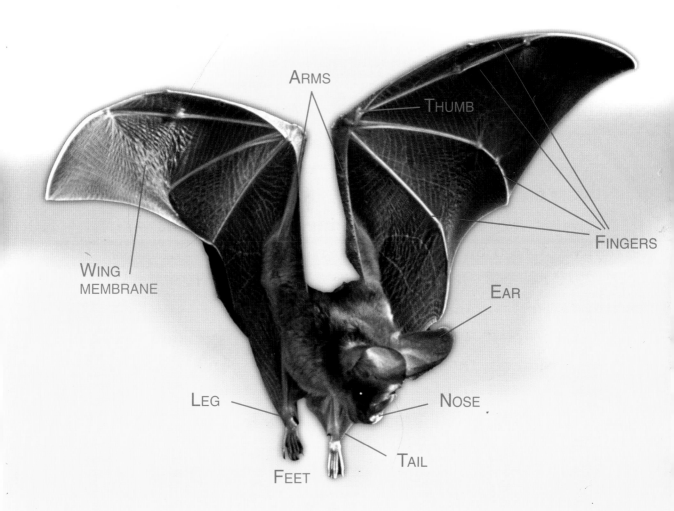

ARMS

THUMB

FINGERS

WING MEMBRANE

EAR

LEG

NOSE

FEET

TAIL

SENSES

Fringe-lipped bats have good eyesight and excellent hearing. They use their large ears to hunt frogs. The bats find frogs by listening for their mating calls.

Male frogs call to attract a mate. Fringe-lipped bats hear the frog calling, swoop down, and grab it with their teeth! The bats hear so well they can tell poisonous frogs from nonpoisonous frogs just by their call. They can also tell which frogs are too big to eat.

Fringe-lipped bats also use echolocation when they are hunting. To use this sense, bats make high-pitched sounds from their throat or from their nose. These sound waves go out and bounce off an object such as a tree, building, or insect.

Bats sense the echo wave as it comes back. They use the echo wave to tell how far away something is. The echo waves also tell bats how big the objects are.

Fringe-lipped bats use echolocation to "see" the area around a frog they hear. That way they can adjust their flight to grab the frog but not run into a nearby tree!

Sound wave sent out by bat

Echo wave received by bat

DEFENSE

Fringe-lipped bats are good at avoiding poisonous frogs when hunting **prey**. But, the bats must avoid other **predators** that prey on them. Fringe-lipped bats are perfect-sized snacks for owls and opossums.

Humans are not natural predators of bats. Fringe-lipped bats have been found to be curious and friendly toward humans. They also have been found to be very intelligent. In fact, researchers believe bats are among the world's smartest **mammals**.

One scientist learned just how smart fringe-lipped bats can be. He trained some of the bats to come to his hand and to fly wherever he pointed. He even trained them to start flying at the sound of a movie camera! The bats learned their new tricks quickly. It took the scientist only a few hours to train them.

As these fringe-lipped bats leave their roost, they must watch for predators that can snatch them out of the air!

FOOD

Fringe-lipped bats hunt by flying low through the forest. They find wet areas such as ponds and slow-running streams where frogs live. Then, they hang from nearby branches and wait. From there, the bats listen for the frogs to begin their mating calls.

When a frog makes its mating call, the bat dives down and grabs it. The bats' favorite snack is the Tungara frog. They also like to eat mud-puddle frogs and pug-nosed tree frogs. One researcher watched a fringe-lipped bat catch six frogs in just an hour!

To defend themselves, the frogs watch the sky for approaching bats. On clear nights the frogs can call loudly. If the bats hear the frogs and come to catch them, the frogs will see the bats in the moonlight. Then, the frogs stop calling so the bats can't find them.

On cloudy nights the frogs can't see the bats coming because there is no moonlight. So they do not call for mates on cloudy nights. This defense keeps the frogs from being eaten. But, it also keeps them from finding a mate. Since fringe-lipped bats cannot easily catch silent frogs, sometimes they will eat insects and fruits.

This fringe-lipped bat has just caught a frog for supper!

BABIES

Researchers have found baby fringe-lipped bats throughout the year. They believe that fringe-lipped bats that live in different regions have babies at different times of the year because of their area's climate.

Mother fringe-lipped bats have only one baby a year. Bat babies are called pups. Bat pups are born fairly well developed. This gives them a better chance of survival.

Mother fringe-lipped bats feed their pups with milk. Mother bats usually leave their pups while they go out and hunt. When a mother returns, she finds her pup by its special smell and squeak sound.

Bat pups can live on their own after about six weeks. Then, they become part of the **ecosystem**, and the life cycle begins again.

A mother fringe-lipped bat with her newborn pup

GLOSSARY

carnivore - an animal or plant that eats meat.

culvert - a drainage tunnel that runs crosswise under roads, sidewalks, and railroads.

ecosystem (EE-koh-sihs-tuhm) - a community of organisms and their environment.

isolate - to separate from something.

mammal - an animal with a backbone that nurses its young with milk.

membrane - a thin, easily bent layer of animal tissue.

muzzle - an animal's nose and jaws.

nocturnal (nahk-TUHR-nuhl) - active at night.

order - a group that scientists use to classify similar plants or animals. It ranks above a family and below a class.

pollinate - when birds and insects transfer pollen from one flower or plant to another.

predator - an animal that kills and eats other animals.

prey - animals that are eaten by other animals; also, the act of seizing prey.

roost - a place, such as a cave or a tree, where bats rest during the day; also, to perch.

species (SPEE-sheez) - a kind or type.

wingspan - the distance from one wing tip to the other when the wings are spread.

WEB SITES

To learn more about fringe-lipped bats, visit ABDO Publishing Company on the World Wide Web at **www.abdopub.com**. Web sites about bats are featured on our Book Links page. These links are routinely monitored and updated to provide the most current information available.

INDEX